Teachers' legal rights and responsibilities

A guide for trainee teachers
and those new to the profession

Teachers' legal rights and responsibilities

A guide for trainee teachers and those new to the profession

Jon Berry

UNIVERSITY OF HERTFORDSHIRE PRESS

First published in Great Britain in 2007 by
University of Hertfordshire Press
College Lane
Hatfield
Hertfordshire AL10 9AB

Second edition 2010
Third edition 2013

British Library Cataloguing in Publication Data
A catalogue record for this book is available from the British Library

ISBN 978-1-909291-09-6

Design by Arthouse Publishing Solutions
Cover design by John Robertshaw
Printed in Great Britain by Henry Ling Ltd

All advice in this guide pertains to the law as it affects schools in England and Wales only. Although there are occasions when legislation in these countries varies, nothing dealt with in these pages is significantly affected by these differences.

Contents

Abbreviations

DfE	Department for Education
EHRC	Equality and Human Rights Commission
LA	Local Authority
LEA	Local Education Authority
NQT	Newly qualified teacher
NSPCC	National Society for the Prevention of Cruelty to Children
NUT	National Union of Teachers
OFSTED	Office for Standards in Education
STPCD	*School Teachers' Pay and Conditions Document*
SEN	Special educational needs

Acknowledgements

Illustrations by Tim Sanders (www.timonline.info) apart from page 3 by Rosie Nieper.

Many thanks to colleagues at the National Union of Teachers, particularly Amanda Brown, for their expertise and guidance.

I'm hugely grateful to all those teachers and those training to enter the profession for allowing me to pick their brains about their concerns and preoccupations in this area and for their illuminating remarks.

Foreword

I am delighted to have the opportunity to write this foreword and, in doing so, to endorse the comments of my late predecessor as General Secretary of the NUT, Steve Sinnott. This guide to the extensive and detailed subject of education and the law will be of considerable interest to teachers and to all those who are variously affected by its complexities and nuances. Jon Berry's experience both in the classroom and as a representative of teachers in a local education authority enables him to identify and explain effectively the legal framework within which teachers work.

Since moving into Higher Education, Jon has continued to demonstrate his commitment to meeting the needs of teachers in the classroom, as is evident in this guide. The guide promotes a better understanding of teachers' rights, duties and responsibilities, which many teachers have neither the time nor the technical knowledge to glean from a direct reading of complex and jargon-ridden regulations and acts of Parliament.

Although the written word cannot be a substitute for expert and specialist advice and representation of the kind that the National Union of Teachers provides, I am sure that this guide will add significantly to the profession's understanding of a challenging but important subject.

Christine Blower
General Secretary
National Union of Teachers

Preface to the third edition

Since the publication of the first edition of this book in 2007 the world of education – which shifts quickly enough at the best of times – has undergone changes that have made some of what was written then seem positively prehistoric. At that time, the advances in digital technology that are now part of the fabric of everyday life were not central to people's working and social existences. One of the ways that this is reflected in this third edition is the greater prominence given to the way in which social networking and digital communication have had an impact on the lives of teachers and their students.

There have also been huge changes in the way in which schools are controlled and governed, with the most obvious feature of this being the growth of academies. Although this has not as yet resulted in huge changes in the interpretation of teachers' pay and conditions, it has meant that I have had to be careful about any assumption that the statutory document which has long been the principal source of reference on these matters – the *School Teachers' Pay and Conditions Document* (STPCD) – is being universally applied.

Keeping up with what the nation's principal education ministry is called would have any writer in this field chasing his tail; this is the Department for Education's fourth renaming since 1995 when it changed its name from ... yes, you guessed it, the Department for Education. Apologies, therefore, if it is called anything different by the time this edition goes to print.

Finally, a quick reminder that this is not a reference book and neither is it a comprehensive guide; it is deliberately designed to be a quick read with the intention of putting people in the picture. In the statistically unlikely event of an individual needing serious legal advice, that person's first port of call must be the school or regional union rep. Much of the purpose of this volume is to stop matters even reaching that point.

Jon Berry
February 2013
j.berry@herts.ac.uk

What this guide sets out to do

Whether you are a teacher setting out on your professional career, or you've been teaching for some time, I hope that this guide will prove useful to you. There is no need for a teacher to be a legal expert, but every teacher should understand the basis of what the law requires in respect of education.

It is worth beginning with a word of caution – and a sense of perspective.

In their working lives, most teachers will have no serious brush with the law in regard to their professional duties. It is true that many of us will work in challenging circumstances and with difficult individuals, but that does not mean that even the most difficult situation will end up with you, as a teacher, facing legal action or prosecution. Such cases are extremely rare and should not colour the way in which we approach this subject. This sense of perspective is essential and I shall be reinforcing it throughout the guide.

This guide will not answer all of your individual questions: no publication of this size could hope to cover every eventuality that besets teachers in their day-to-day work. What I hope to do is provide a clear working guide that will enable teachers to protect themselves in the most effective way possible, that is, to be forewarned and forearmed and so prevent difficult situations arising in the first place. (Needless to say, any teacher who embarks upon working with young people without having joined a trade union or professional association should not, in my view, think about leaving the house unaccompanied, never mind take charge of a class of any sort.)

The guide emphasises that teachers have rights as well as responsibilities. This may have become a rather unfashionable point to make, but just as the emphasis on rights could, in the view of some mid-range tabloid newspapers, have a potentially detrimental effect on how matters work, an over-emphasis on responsibilities without this balance can be equally harmful.

In this age of immediate access to information and documentation, I have not reproduced legislation in full except where it is useful to do so. Unfortunately, it does have to be said that some of those sites that previously provided teachers with useful summaries and information fell foul of a rather rapid – and some would say somewhat rushed and indiscriminate – review of policy by the incoming government in May 2010. Some of that information can now be found at the website of the Department for Education (www.education.gov.uk) which does provide links to most of the areas covered in this guide.

The website of the National Union of Teachers at www.nut.org.uk gives advice, information and contacts for a wide range of issues affecting teachers, including who to contact in times of difficulty. The websites of other teacher organisations may offer similar services.

Professional duties

You may have seen the t-shirt, reproduced below, cheerily sported by some devoted teachers, the front of which lists a whole range of jobs from form-filler to musician, accountant to pencil sharpener, and which finishes with the rather weary exhortation to 'just call me a teacher'.

Many teachers assume this mantle of utter dedication and commitment and are happy and proud to do so. On the other hand, you may well come across plenty of grumpy old men and women who will be equally proud to tell

Administrator, Social Worker, Coat Finder, Arbitrator, Government Directive Reader, Curriculum Implementer, Artistic Director, Form Filler, Language Specialist, Pencil Sharpener, Accountant, Musician, Fundraiser, Report Writer, Nose Wiper, Public Relations Officer, Petty Cash Clerk, Examiner, Surrogate Parent, Walking Encyclopaedia Scapegoat . . . . But you can just call me a TEACHER!

you that their job is just to teach the little so-and-so's and that at that point their professional commitment has been fulfilled.

Defining the extent of what teachers are expected to do, the range of their responsibilities, has been, to say the least, a tricky business for many years. During the industrial disputes of the 1980s, many teachers withdrew from activities which they regarded as coming under the umbrella of 'goodwill' and, as a reaction to this, the government of the time attempted to stipulate more exactly the hours and extent of teachers' duties. Despite the fact that this legislation, largely unaltered, still forms the basis of teachers' duties, there is still confusion, uncertainty and a good deal of unchallenged folklore about what it is, precisely, that teachers have a legal obligation to know and do.

The Teachers' Standards applicable from 2012 state that 'teachers must have an understanding of, and always act within, the statutory frameworks which set out their professional duties and responsibilities'. Notwithstanding various minor changes to this phraseology over the years, this standard has remained much the same and it is difficult to imagine that this fundamental – and non-contentious – requirement will be altered in any way.

But if teachers need to be aware of the statutory frameworks within which they operate, where can this information be found?

All basic information relating to teachers' pay and their conditions of service can be found in the *School Teachers' Pay and Conditions Document* (STPCD), which is published annually and is available online at the Department for Education (DfE) website. This is not exactly bedtime reading, but is still a fairly accessible document which clearly lays out teachers' obligations in terms of the hours and days when they must be available, pay scales and basic duties. Considering the fact that it contains so much information useful to teachers, it is slightly surprising that so few of us have read it, but it does provide a clear and authoritative reference point – and one that might well have proved useful to our t-shirt wearer, stipulating as it does that many of the routine administrative tasks undertaken by teachers in the past are now definitely precluded from their duties.

Does STPCD apply in academies? The stark answer is that there is no obligation for the owners and controllers of academies to adhere to it, at least for newly appointed staff: one of the principal ideological drivers behind the academies project is to liberate those who run them from what could be perceived as unnecessary bureaucratic control. If, as will currently be the case for many teachers, you have continued employment in a school after its transition to an academy, you will still be operating under STPCD. If not, there is no obligation on your employer to recognise the document. In reality, however, most academies have applied STPCD or something very similar as it is not in their interest to either reinvent the wheel or to place themselves out of step with neighbouring schools.

It goes without saying that the vast majority of teachers enter the profession with, at the very least, some sense of duty and service and, as a consequence, do not wish to see bureaucratic restrictions and petty rules dictate how they interact with the children in their charge. This is perfectly understandable and, indeed, even desirable. Few teachers count the hours or measure their commitment to school and pupils in the way that workers in some other trades and professions may choose to do. Nevertheless, in ensuring that they fulfil their legal obligations and duties, it is equally important for teachers to be aware of how legislation also affords them protection and security: to be acquainted with such matters is not to be petty or confrontational, but is a way of ensuring that teachers' many responsibilities are balanced by their proper rights.

The duty of care to pupils

The story below became something of a rallying cry for the 'political correctness gone mad' brigade a few years ago and has passed into Health and Safety mythology:

> A headmaster has introduced safety goggles for his pupils in a bid to stop the local council banning games of conkers in the playground. Shaun Halfpenny, the head of Cummersdale Primary School in Cumbria, feared the game would be banned after he read a council memo warning schools about dangerous break-time activities. It was suggested that youngsters could suffer eye injuries if struck by flying pieces of conker produced when the winner smashes the opponent's conker.   *Guardian*, 4 October 2004

One can only imagine the spluttering outrage, even of readers of liberal newspapers, when stories like the one above hit the headlines. As it happens, the head teacher here had arranged for some kids to pose in goggles as his own protest against burdensome health and safety regulations, but why let the truth get in the way of a good story? All the same, have we really reached the point where sensible individuals can consider banning robust games because of fear of freak accidents, or even the everyday bumps and scratches of childhood? Is this really what the concept of 'duty of care' has come to?

As we shall see in a moment, the answer is definitely not, but as a starting point – and without becoming too pedantic – it is worth considering what we mean by 'the law'.

Teachers' legal responsibilities derive from three sources:

- The common law duty of care, which is the body of law derived from court decisions over the years (as opposed to law which has been determined by Parliament and set down in statutes)
- The statutory duty of care arising from the Children Act 1989
- Their contractual duties as laid out, for example, in the *School Teachers' Pay and Conditions Document*

The common law duty of care

Ask most teachers what they understand by the application of duty of care and their response will almost certainly contain the phrase '*in loco parentis*', in recognition of the fact that they are acting in place of a parent. This definition is only useful up to a point, stemming as it does from an 1893 court ruling that 'the schoolmaster is bound to take such care of his pupils as a careful father would'. Leaving aside the quaint gender bias of this ancient ruling, it is fairly obvious that such a judgement is fraught with potential difficulties of interpretation, not least of which is to consider whether 'a careful father' would, for example, allow his offspring to climb on PE equipment in the gym, peer over the edge of a muddy pond or, indeed, play conkers.

As a consequence, a more refined ruling in 1955 stated that 'a balance must be struck between the meticulous supervision of children every moment of the day and the desirable object of encouraging sturdy independence as they grow up'. It is this ruling which corresponds, of course, to the way in which most people would go about the business of supervising children, whether this be in the classroom or in the playground of their local park. By 1962 the courts had recognised that the 'standard of care' expected from a teacher was held to be that of a person exhibiting the responsible mental qualities of a *parent in the circumstances of a school, rather than home life*. The distinction is an important one, acknowledging as it does that the 'sturdy independence' of a child is to be encouraged, and that classroom activities may present the occasional risk.

What does this mean in real terms for the teacher preparing for an experiment in science, a nature walk or a game of rugby? The critical thing to remember is that as long as a teacher has applied the ordinary skills of a

Professional Bodies

Most subject and curriculum areas have their own professional bodies that offer advice and information on a whole range of things. Only some of these are listed below, but such organisations exist for most subject areas.

The Association for Science Education • www.ase.org.uk

The Association for Physical Education • www.afpe.org.uk

The Geographical Association • www.geography.org.uk

RE Today Services (run by the charity Christian Education Movement) • www.retoday.org.uk

The National Association of Advisers and Inspectors in Design and Technology • www.naaidt.org.uk

competent professional and that the teacher has acted in accordance with the views of a reputable body of opinion within their profession, the duty of care will have been met.

In an age where we can barely turn on the TV without seeing advertising claiming that huge sums of compensation are available for accidents and mishaps, it is hardly surprising that many teachers remain a bit jumpy about where they stand. Broadly speaking, however, individual teachers have little to fear just as long as they apply their professional judgement, experience and training, and can demonstrate that their actions were taken with the best interests of the children in mind. The law will protect individual teachers in almost all cases – but cannot make allowances for any stupidity, negligence or fecklessness on their part. Whether or not an individual teacher is found to be negligent will depend entirely upon whether an accident or mishap could reasonably have been foreseen; if teachers take reasonable (there's that word again) steps to ensure students' safety, the likelihood of their being found negligent is very slim indeed.

It is worth bearing in mind that in those rare cases where a teacher is found to be individually negligent, and where an injury occurs to a pupil as a consequence of this, compensation could be due to the child, this compensation being payable by the teacher's employer. Nevertheless, this could have serious consequences that could even result in dismissal for the teacher concerned,

following the implementation of disciplinary procedures.

The final thing to consider in this section about the common law duty of care is collective or institutional failure or negligence, in which cases it is the school as an institution, rather than any particular individual, that is responsible for failing to execute its duties. This is most commonly manifested in the area of bullying, or as the result of dangerous or disruptive behaviour that goes unchallenged. In the event of a complaint from, for example, the victim of bullying, the extent to which the failure is collective or individual would be a matter that could be contested.

In summary: the law does *not* protect you if you have been stupid, lazy or wilfully negligent, but if you have acted sensibly and in accordance with proper, professional procedures, you should have nothing to worry about.

The statutory duty of care

Teachers also have responsibilities under the Children Act 1989, which places duties upon those who care for children.

The Children Act represented a shift in legislation which brought to the fore a more child-focused approach to the law, asserting that the needs of the child are paramount. The Act declares that a person with care of a child may do all that is reasonable in the circumstances for the purposes of safeguarding or promoting the welfare of the child. As we shall see in later sections, this has ramifications for what a teacher may or may not do, especially in situations where a child is at risk of harm. Nevertheless, the main point is to emphasise that the welfare of the child must be of prime importance when considering our duty of care.

The contractual duty of care

Although school life can present teachers and pupils with situations that may, on occasion, be potentially dangerous, the plain fact is that most children do not spend their school day abseiling down the Art block, mixing up Semtex or tramping over Dartmoor without a compass. The majority of time on the majority of days is spent in perfectly safe classrooms engaged in perfectly safe activities. It is in these ordinary, everyday circumstances that teachers will fulfil the duty of care arising from their contract of employment, the terms of which have to comply with the *School Teachers' Pay and Conditions Document* already referred to.

The STPCD sets out clearly and unequivocally the main terms of employment of all teachers. Matters such as contracted hours and the number of days you should be available for work are properly outlined. Pay scales and the range of duties are also included. The STPCD is revised annually and takes effect in September of each year.

In concise terms this means that, unsurprisingly, teachers have to carry out their professional duties as circumstances may require under the reasonable direction of the head teacher of the school. In doing so, teachers are charged with promoting the general progress and wellbeing of individual pupils or of any class or group of pupils assigned to them.

As well as these duties, teachers' duty of care extends to maintaining good order and discipline and safeguarding their pupils' health and safety, both when they are on school premises and engaged in authorised school activities elsewhere. Teachers are also contracted to attend assemblies (although there are exceptions allowing withdrawal on religious grounds) and register attendance.

All of the above should strike you, with good cause, as absolutely obvious. After all, that's what teachers do: teach, keep order, keep a general eye on the welfare, health and safety of their pupils, and encourage them to fulfil their academic and personal potential. It cannot be emphasised too strongly that, in the everyday course of events, teachers who prepare lessons thoroughly, teach their classes with energy and enthusiasm, and mark and assess their pupils' work punctually and systematically will be fulfilling their common law, statutory and contractual duties of care to pupils to the letter.

Finally, a word about 'reasonableness'. Both in the execution of their own duties and in the definition of those duties by head teachers, the idea of reasonableness keeps reappearing. It goes without saying that lawyers grow fat on the debates arising from what is reasonable and what is not in any given set of circumstances; no legislation – let alone a guide of this sort – can allow for all eventualities. The test of what is reasonable is at the centre of many a wrangle, both in the courts and in your staffroom, and the very use of the term implies that there must be flexibility and a degree of broadness in its implementation. Deciding what is reasonable, particularly in difficult and fraught situations, is not always a clear-cut matter. However, what is critical at those times when disputes arise is that all parties enter into sensible dialogue with a view to speedy and effective resolution. For teachers this will almost certainly mean turning to your trade union or professional association for advice, and to leave yourself unprotected in this area is at best careless and, at worst, downright stupid.

Living – and teaching
– in the digital age

Of the many societal changes that have had an impact on teachers' working conditions, the use of digital technology is one of the most important. For most teachers and school students, the use of such technology to enhance learning has brought enormous benefits. Increasingly, technological knowledge and expertise – from both sides of the teacher's desk – have improved time in school for everyone. However, as we are all aware, there are also dangers and pitfalls in this new age.

I first knew the world was changing some years ago when I had to represent a teacher whose ICT-savvy Year 10 group had established a website which, for the sake of argument, we will call www.mrjonesisafool.com – although, of course, it wasn't quite as mild as that. Since then we've been treated to the more strident RateMyTeachers.com and, in a development that is now relatively widespread, the use of Facebook by young people and, alarmingly, their parents, to comment on and openly gossip about school- and teacher-related matters. Balanced against this is the fact that for decades schoolchildren have been scratching such messages into desks or scrawling them on walls – but putting them on the worldwide web is a rather different matter. Although it has long been the inalienable right of all pupils to moan and gripe about their teachers' various shortfalls, such conversations were limited to themselves and a few mates and soon forgotten – not committed to a social networking site and viewable by all.

In the vast majority of such cases, it's probably worth remembering that insulting, abusive behaviour by pupils – or parents – towards teachers should be dealt with as a routine matter of school discipline and protocol. Although this modern form of graffiti may be on a screen rather than on the bike-shed wall, school leaders should pursue such behaviour thoroughly and vigorously. If you're the victim of abusive comments on such sites, your first recourse should be to your head teacher. Beyond this, all social networking sites have facilities to report abusive comments and most of them do pursue offenders. Of course, should such comments infringe the law of the land, then there is the possibility of police intervention, for which precedent now exists. The DfE, along with organisations such as the UK Council for Child Internet Safety and KidSMART, have produced excellent guidance on this aspect of school life including model Acceptable Use policies which clearly delineate boundaries and sanctions.

History also tells us that many teachers, before settling into the quiet respectability of their profession, may well have had their wilder moments: it's just that no one had the capacity to stick them on YouTube for all and sundry to enjoy for ever after. The uploading of indiscreet footage can make things very tricky for teachers. If, as in one or two lurid cases of late, the behaviour predated the teacher's training or entry into the profession, employers have no recourse to act – although it may, of course, be cringingly embarrassing for the teachers involved. If such events happen *after* taking up a post or training, then, depending on the circumstances, a school may decide to pursue matters – and it's at that point that you must contact your union rep. In terms of how teachers use their own social networking sites, the best advice is to use the highest possible level of discretion and privacy, working on the premise that if something malicious could happen, then it possibly will. You should also be aware that some employers will now, as a matter of course, view your profile on Facebook and other sites.

A further area that leaves teachers vulnerable to problems is the use of emails and texts to communicate with students and parents. Although there are obvious advantages to this, it is an area fraught with problems – as anyone caught in a blazing email argument will recognise. The inability to capture tone in a quickfire email and the ambiguity that is so typical of many texts could leave all parties exposed. The strongest possible advice here is to follow your school's established protocols and advice for the use of such communications. If no such guidelines exist, then you should completely avoid this particular means of establishing contact. It goes without saying that entering into private communication with a pupil in this way is an act of folly.

Similarly, the use of, and attitude to, mobile phones in school varies greatly. Find out what procedures and policies exist in your school so that you can be sure that your pupils – and you – stick to them. As with so many of the issues discussed in this guide, sticking unequivocally to your school's policies will provide you with plenty of protection in practically every instance.

Activities out of school

Children should be able to go on exciting school trips that broaden their horizons. Education Secretary, Michael Gove, 2011

Memories of our school trips stay with us. Learning outside the classroom brings the curriculum to life and is essential to our children's development. Employment Secretary, Chris Grayling, 2011

For most people, school trips form some of the most enduring memories of their schooldays. As a pupil you may not have embarked upon them thinking that your education was being enhanced at every given moment: the stronger likelihood is that you spent at least a week beforehand sorting out the pecking order on the coach. Nevertheless, there is a clear and unchallenged understanding that such journeys, whether they involve a brief stroll around the local neighbourhood or a week's exchange in a school halfway across the globe, are of enormous educational, academic and social value to pupils and staff alike. It is also encouraging that government ministers, like those cited above, clearly recognise the need to 'dispel myths about legal action and encourage all schools to ditch unnecessary paperwork, ensuring that precautions are proportionate to the risks involved' (DfE advice, 2011).

It is regrettable, therefore, that the occasional tragic mishap should have generated nervousness and unwillingness among a (very) few schools and teachers to embark upon such activities. This anxiety has, to a great extent, been reinforced by a perception that the paperwork involved in organising such events is so onerous as to be a deterrent in itself. These two elements are, of course, linked. As a reaction to the unfounded fear of an enormous lawsuit in the case of negligence, some schools do go about a belt-and-braces approach to risk assessment, which many teachers both find time-consuming and regard as unnecessary. Such an approach, as we shall see from the following paragraphs, largely arises from a misunderstanding of what is really necessary to demonstrate that a proper duty of care has been exercised. (On a purely practical note, it is also worth remembering that many schools now employ a non-teacher in the role of Educational Visit Coordinator, or similar title, which removes the burden of this bureaucratic task from teachers.)

So how do individual teachers, as well as schools, protect themselves against legal liability? Let us start by reminding ourselves of two concepts with which, by now, we should be very familiar: negligence and reasonableness.

Unless it can be proven that an injury sustained by a pupil is as a direct result of *individual* negligence then a teacher is not liable.

Vicarious liability

On the face of it, this rather grand-sounding legal concept seems to be a 'get out of jail free' card for the individual teacher. What it means is that in case of accident or injury that could lead to legal liability, it is the employer – either the Local Education Authority (LEA) or the governing body, depending on the nature of the school involved – rather than the employee who is liable. This may sound all well and good for the individual teacher, but it is highly likely that any employer who is claimed against will pursue the teacher through the school's own disciplinary procedures should that employer believe the teacher involved has acted carelessly or imprudently.

Technically speaking, when it comes to voluntary activities out of school it would, indeed, be the teacher who is the named defendant in a case of potential negligence, which is why there is a longstanding agreement that employers have to obtain insurance cover for such activities, giving the same protection as if there were vicarious liability.

It is always worth remembering that there is no law or procedure in existence which will protect individuals who have acted without the due care and attention required in a given situation.

There are a number of clear and obvious steps that any teacher can take in order to demonstrate that he or she is fulfilling their duty of care – and many of these steps need to be taken at the preparatory stage of a planned activity.

- Where it is relevant to do so, consult the advice given by relevant subject associations.
- Read the advice given by the Department for Education (www.dfe.gov.uk).
- Read any Local Authority advice available.
- Read your school's policy, guidance and advice.

By taking the steps above, you should have a clear indication of such matters as the staffing ratio suggested, the level of risk assessment required, and the degree of supervision needed given the particular activity to be undertaken. By acting upon this advice, you will have gone a very long way towards demonstrating that you have fulfilled your duty of care.

Sensible teachers know that the best way of dealing with any problem in the classroom is to prevent it from actually arising in the first place. The same applies to an out-of-school activity: if you feel that it has been inadequately prepared for, is poorly organised and the level of preparation is not consistent with the advice given by the bodies mentioned above, then you should refuse to participate. Although the ultimate responsibility for any liability rests with your employer, it should go without saying that it is foolish to place yourself in a situation where you believe that inadequate preparation has taken place.

So ... let us assume that all necessary preparation has been adequately completed: what about the situation once the activity is under way? Depending, of course, on the activity itself, the very point of many out-of-school events is to encourage the 'sturdy independence' of which the law speaks. How do teachers do this without either mollycoddling the pupils in their care or setting themselves impossibly high standards when it comes to adequate supervision of potentially hazardous activities?

Once again, it is important to go back to what is reasonable. The standard of care required from teachers is that which, from an objective point of view, can reasonably be expected from teachers generally applying skill and awareness of the problems, needs and susceptibilities of children. The law expects the teacher to do what a caring parent would do whilst bearing in mind that taking responsibility for twenty pupils is entirely different from looking after a family. The legal duty of care expected of the individual is what a caring teaching profession would expect of itself.

In real terms what does this mean? Can a teacher, for example, allow a small group of Year 6 pupils to explore a particular exhibition in a museum unsupervised? Should a group of Year 10s visiting an exhibition or careers fair be set free in an unfamiliar city during their lunch break? At what time should a group of Year 12s be told to be back in their Paris hotel? Unsurprisingly, there are no clear-cut answers here and that is because, ultimately, any teacher has to apply professional judgement consistent with each particular case whilst, most importantly, taking into account their knowledge and understanding of the abilities and capabilities of any given group of pupils. What is of paramount importance is that an individual teacher is confident that he or she has taken all reasonable steps to avoid exposing pupils to dangers which are foreseeable and with which those pupils may not be expected to cope. It is critical that the level of risk is commensurate with what that teacher knows about the groups or individuals involved. It is a pretty trite thing to say, but not all twelve-year-olds are the same, and it is up to the teacher to make judgements in the light of this. It is also vital that parents and carers are apprised as fully as possible of the arrangements for any visit.

What of those pupils who refuse to obey instructions, or who disregard advice or important information? Fundamentally, the situation here is little different from that in the classroom. It is a rather foolish teacher who believes that an instruction given once in a classroom will immediately be acted upon by the entire class: points will need to be repeated and certain groups or individuals will need to be targeted for extra emphasis. Occasionally, different arrangements will need to be made for groups or individuals with particular needs, whether or not their inability to cope stems from wilfulness or lack of basic understanding. The same principles apply to out-of-school activities. Teachers need to take into account that some challenging or unco-

Supervisors

On certain trips and for certain activities, supervision of pupils will be handed over to specialist guides and instructors. Technically, pupils are still under the direct supervision of the teacher in these circumstances. It goes without saying, therefore, that the credentials and qualifications of such instructors need to have been thoroughly checked and verified – preferably, of course, as part of the planning for the event and not at the time itself. If you are in any way uncertain about the qualifications or expertise of such instructors, pupils should be withdrawn from the activity.

operative behaviour may take place, and this needs to be seen in the context of the potential consequences of pupils disobeying rules and instructions. Balanced against this is the need to give pupils a degree of latitude consistent with what teachers know about their level of personal responsibility.

Given that practically all of this seems to be plain old common sense, you could be forgiven for asking yourself what all the fuss is about in relation to out-of-school activities. Don't misinterpret this: there is no doubt that for all their evident value, school trips are just as exhausting as they are rewarding for the average teacher! There is no suggestion that there is nothing to be learnt from the occasional tragic event, and many of us engaged in out-of-school activities can probably think of instances where we were moments from potential disaster. Nevertheless, as far as your legal responsibilities are concerned, these are the questions you need to ask yourself in order to ensure that you have fulfilled your legal obligations:

• Have I read and acted upon all of the relevant advice: subject association, DfE, LA, school policy?
• Have the credentials and qualifications of any external supervisors been verified?
• Are the planned activities commensurate with what I know about the abilities and level of responsibility of the pupils involved?
• Are parents and carers aware of all foreseeable arrangements for the trip?

Even experienced teachers will need to discuss some of these issues with colleagues before embarking upon such activities, and with teaching, as

with everything else, there are no risk-free activities. However, careful and thorough preparation, along with a clear understanding of what 'duty of care' really means, will protect you when taking part in one of the best and most memorable elements of your teaching career.

Health and safety at work

A press story is saying that health and safety is the barrier to children enjoying everyday activities such as playing conkers, using skipping ropes or climbing trees. Skipping, playing conkers and football and climbing trees are all important activities which help children to have fun and learn about handling risk at the same time. There is no health and safety legislation which bans these activities; in fact HSE is on record as encouraging schools to allow these activities to go ahead.

From the website of the Health and Safety Executive, 2012

Quite how legislation introduced to ensure that workers can be suitably protected as they go about their day-to-day business has attracted almost universal opprobrium from sections of the media is something of a mystery. Nevertheless it has, unfortunately, become somewhat commonplace in certain circles to equate health and safety with petty and obstructive behaviour. Given that adherence to basic health and safety principles can be a matter of life and death, it is a shame that it often receives such an unfortunate and unjustified press.

The Health and Safety at Work Act 1974 is the principal piece of legislation dictating what is required in this important area of school life. It is critical to remember that prime responsibility under the Act rests with the employer rather than the employee. In the first instance this means that employers have to ensure they have taken reasonable care of the health and safety of employees and others on their premises. Of course, this has implications for you as an employee: should you feel that such reasonable care is *not* being taken, it is a matter of *duty* for you to pursue this, either through a line manager or union representative. Failure to act on an issue that could result in injury to a pupil, where early intervention or reporting on a teacher's part might have prevented this, could in some circumstances point to individual negligence. As ever, in your relationship to the law as an employee, what is vitally important is that you act in a proper and professional way, following such advice as is available: by doing so, you will place responsibility firmly at the door of the employer, where it properly rests.

Before we look at exactly who is responsible for what, let us pause for a moment and think about what health and safety issues mean in the daily context of school life. I have already made fleeting reference to what is currently called the 'compensation culture'. Comical manifestations of this can be seen in advertisements on TV where some hapless soul re-enacts the tumble that resulted in their winning a huge sum of money in compensation. As crude as these adverts are, they do encapsulate a basic truth about health and safety: minor spillages, uncollected rubbish, faulty fittings and unchecked appliances cause preventable accidents that can result in injury. To protect yourself under the law, it is your duty to report these apparently inconsequential matters to whoever is charged with dealing with them. In almost all schools there will also be a recording system for accidents and you must familiarise yourself with this too and use it in the proper way.

So, although basic responsibility does, indeed, rest with the employer, this does not exonerate the employee in any way whatsoever. The Act is entirely clear that all employees have to take care of the health and safety of themselves as well as of others who may be affected by their acts or omissions at work. So, don't ...

- prop the door open with the fire extinguisher
- put the chair on the table and then stand on it so that you can just finish off that final bit of the display
- bring in your electrical extension lead from home to get your laptop in the correct position
- just dump that box of books by the fire door for five minutes

Sound familiar? (And in case you think you detect a degree of smugness, I have been guilty on all counts.) Section 8 of the Act tells us clearly that it is unlawful to interfere with or misuse, either intentionally or recklessly, anything which has been provided for the purposes of health and safety. Moreover, the Act demands that teachers should act with reasonable care at all times and apply good sense to everything they do. It goes without saying that the examples above – and all of the other well-meaning but slightly idiotic things that teachers may do – do not fit into the category of 'good sense', and that by acting in such a way, teachers potentially forfeit their protection under the law.

Balanced against this is the fundamental precept that employers have to organise, monitor, control and review how health and safety measures are managed. They also have to assess risks and, most critically, inform their employees of procedures and policies; such policies should be in writing and easily accessible. It is the employee's responsibility to become familiar with these policies and procedures and to act upon them accordingly.

It may sound fanciful to say that in the middle of preparing lessons, marking work, attending meetings and just getting on with your life as a teacher, you should also find the time to locate and read such policies (especially in the whirlwind at the start of your career), but not to do so could be placing yourself in a difficult situation. A few moments spent reading a policy document could save a lot of time and trouble later on.

Discipline

> The children now love luxury. They have bad manners, contempt for authority, they show disrespect to their elders.... They no longer rise when elders enter the room. They contradict their parents, chatter before company, gobble up dainties at the table and are tyrants over their teachers. The young people of today think of nothing but themselves. They have no reverence for parents or old age. They are impatient of all restraint. They talk as if they alone knew everything and what passes for wisdom with us is foolishness with them. As for girls, they are forward, immodest and unwomanly in speech, behaviour and dress.
>
> Socrates, 469–399 BC

A teaching colleague of mine once claimed that when asked about his job at parties he would say he was a cobbler, on the grounds that he was fairly certain this was an occupation about which his fellow guests would not have an instant – and probably ill-informed – viewpoint. Whether or not this strategy was effective (or, indeed, true – I never actually saw it in action), it's an illuminating anecdote. Everyone has a view about teaching, and *absolutely* everyone has a view about discipline or behaviour management in schools.

Broadly speaking, the consensus is that there has been a gradual deterioration over the years, and that the rigours of 'good old-fashioned discipline' are a thing of the past. A whole range of TV shows focusing on the need to enforce discipline, rigour and routine in the lives of young people have helped to reinforce this viewpoint, which seems to hanker after a (largely mythical) golden age. There is, of course, no way of making sensible, informed comparisons between generations on this subject, but there is no escaping the fact that the behaviour of pupils remains one of the main – if not *the* main – preoccupation of almost all teachers. Given this, and given that on the issue of classroom control he or she who hesitates is most definitely lost, it is vitally important for teachers to know where they stand as far as the law is concerned.

Firstly, and notwithstanding the mythology of the effective 'clip round the ear' which served previous generations, any form of touching, restraint or force used as a disciplinary measure is entirely unacceptable in any circumstances. There are no exceptions to this, and any teacher who uses such measures will not be protected by the law.

All schools will have a system of procedures for behaviour management: although broadly similar, there may be differences of emphasis and style. The most recent piece of relevant legislation, the Education Act 2011, is unequivocal in its position with regard to the right of teachers to discipline pupils and the support they should receive when attempting to do so, with the minister for schools, Nick Gibb, unambiguously expressing the view that 'the role of the Government is to give schools the freedom and support they need to provide a safe and structured environment in which teachers can teach and children can learn'.

Teachers new to the profession may well regard a school's behaviour management system as one of the principal reasons for choosing to work there, or not. What is important to appreciate is that whatever system a school chooses to employ, that's the one you will have to implement in your day-to-day conduct. Going back to the idea of our contractual duties, this system will be the directive of the head teacher, and putting it into practice will go a long way towards protecting yourself in a legal sense. When teachers find themselves in difficulty in the area of behaviour management, it is often because agreed school procedures have not been followed and a teacher has carried out some ad hoc punishment on the spot and in the heat of the moment.

Perhaps the most contentious area of debate when it comes to the punishment of pupils is that of detention. When that impertinent thirteen-year-old gleefully tells you that you can't put her in detention because you ain't given her twenty-four hours' notice, is she correct? And how long should it be for? And what should pupils be doing in that time? Although most school policies worth their salt will deal with these issues, the law, via Section 550B of the Education Act 1996, is helpful and illuminating.

Perhaps the most surprising thing teachers discover is that the law allows for the detention of pupils at the end of school sessions (and this, of course, need not necessarily mean at the end of the day itself) *without parental consent.*

However, for detention to be put into practice, certain preconditions have to apply.

The first of these is that it must be generally known that the detention of pupils is part of the school's disciplinary system. This must have been made clear to parents and pupils beforehand through whichever means a school chooses to employ, such as newsletters, parents' meetings or information on websites. The critical thing is that everyone must know detention is a sanction used in that particular school.

Secondly, the law is clear that the detention 'must be reasonable in all the circumstances'. Consideration should be taken in relation to age and ability as well as any special needs that pupils may have. Travel arrangements may be a further concern, as well as any religious or cultural issues that may be significant. Any punishments, including tasks set as punishment during the detention, need to be proportionate.

For example, many schools choose not to implement after-school detentions during the winter months when travelling home alone and after dark may be an issue. In these circumstances, should a school choose to use detention as part of its system and should it want such detentions to take place at another time of the day, then as long as this arrangement has been made clear to parents and pupils, it is legitimate to act in this way.

However, do note that teachers' contractual duties as laid out in the *School Teachers' Pay and Conditions Document* also allow for 'a break of reasonable length between school sessions' and so the supervision of such detentions may be an issue in some schools.

The issue of parental consent and the necessity of providing twenty-four hours' notice merit comment because both of these issues are subject to deep-rooted misconceptions. As long as detention is recognised by all parties as part of the school's disciplinary procedures, the need to inform parents of its use becomes unnecessary. Nonetheless, the guidance from the DfE recognises that many schools may wish to inform

Keeping them back for five minutes

Very often, classroom situations arise in which a teacher wants to make a point about lateness, minor disruption or mildly irritating behaviour from a class or an individual and, as a consequence, will threaten to prevent a class from going to break or lunch.
It's nothing like a full-blown detention, but it is a response to an immediate situation that a short, sharp reprimand may resolve. Is this legitimate? Is it a 'detention'?

The answer, as always, lies in the expectations of the school and what is contained in its policies. The law has nothing to say about these impromptu punishments, but the person waiting for their next lesson may well have! Check whether this is part of the school's way of operating before using this approach.

parents as a matter of course but that a short detention after school, where the judgement has been made that a child can get home safely, definitely does not require any such notice.

As with all matters relating to behaviour management, the ultimate responsibility lies with the head teacher. When an individual teacher detains pupils, that teacher is doing so as the person authorised to do so; acting, in other words, as the head teacher's delegate. This is yet another instance where there is no substitute for knowing precisely what is expected from you in accordance with your own school's policies and procedures.

In this section about behaviour management there has been no attempt to delve into the whole area of suspensions and exclusions. For those at the start of their careers such momentous decisions are a long way off. For general information, it will be valuable to read through the material on the DfE website and it is definitely worth knowing your school's policy regarding such measures. However, it would be foolish in the extreme to use the threat of such measures as part of your approach to classroom management and general discipline.

Physical contact and restraint

Physical contact

Coming from a secondary background, I always remember a conversation I had with a group of primary teachers when doing the initial research for this book. A teacher told the rest of the group about a child who regularly came into school in the morning, dumped her bag and coat wherever (in)convenient and came up to give her a cuddle. What, this new teacher wanted to know, was she supposed to do about that? Her concern and slight discomfort stemmed from one of the most popular misconceptions to have dogged the profession in recent years: teachers, apparently, are not to touch pupils under any circumstances. It is, of course, not difficult to see where this misunderstanding may have come from – and it is critically important that teachers understand the legal and professional parameters within which they have to work when it comes to touching pupils – but it certainly is a misunderstanding and one that needs careful unpicking.

Having reached this point in the guide, a number of phrases and principles should now be familiar to you. Of these principles the one that says you should be completely conversant with school policy and practice, under the direction of the head teacher, is paramount. It is just possible that the head teacher of the school in question had issued a directive that staff must not touch, cuddle or comfort children in any way – and if that were the case it would be foolish for any member of staff to disregard that advice. What is more likely, however, is that the head would have issued advice similar to that which appears in various governmental circulars and advisory documents. The current government has been particularly insistent in its efforts to ensure that the myth of no-touching be exposed as such.

It is worth quoting Circular 10/98, which, although some fifteen years old, is still relevant:

There may be occasions where a distressed pupil needs comfort and reassurance which may include physical comforting such as a caring parent would give. Staff should use their discretion in such cases to ensure that what is normal and natural does not become unnecessary and unjustified contact, particularly with the same pupil over a period of time. Where a member of staff has particular concern about the need to provide this type of care and reassurance they should seek the advice of the head teacher. Some staff are likely to come into physical contact with pupils from time to time in the course of their duties. Staff should be aware of the limits within which such contact should properly take place and of the possibility of such contact being misinterpreted.

TeacherNet (now subsumed into the DfE website) amplified the latter part of this advice, which has now found its way into many school and local authority policies:

Physical contact may be misconstrued by a pupil, parent or observer. Touching pupils, including well-intentioned gestures such as putting a hand on the shoulder can, if repeated regularly, lead to serious questions being raised. As a general principle, staff must not make gratuitous physical contact with their pupils. It is particularly unwise to attribute touching to their teaching style or as a way of relating to pupils.

This advice is a long way from a simple 'don't touch' directive, but it is plain to see that it is hedged around with a number of caveats, most of which are blindingly obvious. We're back, once again, to the idea of a caring parent in the circumstances of the school, adherence to policies and advice, and the application of a degree of common sense.

There are also, of course, any number of other occasions where touching, supporting and physically guiding pupils are intrinsic parts of the actual teaching process. In its guidance on the use of reasonable force, the DfE lists the following as examples of 'occasions when physical contact, other than reasonable force, with a pupil is proper and necessary':

- holding the hand of the child at the front/back of the line when going to assembly or when walking together around the school

Council chiefs say they have had no complaints from parents over claims some children in Denbighshire would be kept indoors unless they apply their own sun cream. Vale of Clwyd Assembly Member Ann Jones said one parent had protested to her that her child's school had issued the warning. The council said individual schools and parents should decide whether teachers put cream on young children in the sun. BBC News website, 7 June 2006

The story of the teachers banned from applying sun cream falls, of course, into the 'world gone mad' category so beloved by parts of the media. The position would have been clearer, however, if only things had happened in a perfect world. The schools could, and perhaps should, have alerted parents to the need to supply children with sun cream for outdoor activities during periods of hot weather. Such a communication would also have alerted parents to the fact that, should teachers be concerned that cream had not been applied adequately or correctly – and how many excited six-year-olds might be trusted to have done so? – then they would intervene and do so unless otherwise instructed by the parent or carer. Duty of care would then have been fulfilled and the needs of the child, as well as concerns over health and safety, would have been catered for. It goes without saying, nonetheless, that any sensible and thoughtful teacher would wish to apply sun cream to a child in the presence of another adult.

- when comforting a distressed pupil
- when a pupil is being congratulated or praised
- to demonstrate how to use a musical instrument
- to demonstrate exercises or techniques during PE lessons or sports coaching
- to give first aid

Subject associations can usefully provide more specific advice. The following, for example, from the website of the Child Protection in Sport Unit, gives a flavour of the sort of specific advice that is available:

Physical contact during sport should always be intended to meet the child's needs, NOT the adult's. The adult should only use physical contact if their aim is to:

- develop sports skills or techniques
- treat an injury
- prevent an injury
- meet the requirements of the sport

The adult should explain the reason for the physical contact to the child. Unless the situation is an emergency, the adult should ask the child for permission.

In another example, the online journal of Music Teachers UK directs its readers to the website of the Musicians' Union, which gives the following advice:

Most instrumental teachers may find themselves in situations where they are likely to come into physical contact with their pupils in the course of their duties. All instrumental teachers should be aware of the context in which such contact should properly take place and of the possibility of such contact being misinterpreted. Instrumental teachers working with individual or small groups of pupils are potentially subject to a much greater threat of misinterpretation of such actions, or indeed of malicious allegations. The best advice at all times is for instrumental teachers to avoid physical contact with pupils except when absolutely necessary, and then to ask another adult to be present to observe their actions.

There will be similar examples from all subject associations across the curriculum. The point about this is that as long as teachers comply with the advice given locally (by their school and/or local authority) along with that of a reputable public body (such as recognised associations or trade unions), those teachers will have gone about their business properly and will have fulfilled their duties and obligations to the letter.

None of this, however, condones physical punishment in any way whatsoever. The law here is unequivocal, emphasising that both physical punishment and physical responses to misbehaviour are unacceptable unless they are by way of restraint – which is dealt with below.

Finally on the topic of touching, there are of course many teachers working in special circumstances with children with specialised and complex needs, and for whom the guidance applicable to mainstream schools will often be inadequate. Such teachers will be given particular guidance and training and can also find documentation on the DfE website which addresses this specialist area.

Physical restraint

When it comes to the issue of physical force to restrain pupils who are in danger of harming themselves or others, the current government has been quick to highlight its updated advice on this – although much of it does little more than echo what has been in place for the past twenty years or so. Sometimes such advice, clear and well-intentioned as it is, can sound just a touch comical and strait-laced in its use of understatement. A circular of 1998 advises us that, 'before intervening physically a teacher should, wherever practicable, tell the pupil who is misbehaving to stop and what will happen if he or she does not'.

The advice, difficult as it may be to follow, still holds and is sound and sensible – and we'd all like to think we'd be able to follow it. Despite the fact that the legislation has been dusted down a few times since 1998, the basic principles still pertain and are embedded in the latest DfE advice from 2012. In short, this tells us that the teacher should continue attempting to communicate with the pupil throughout the incident and should make it clear that physical contact or restraint will stop as soon as it ceases to be necessary. We are reminded that a calm and measured approach to a situation is needed and that teachers should never give the impression they have lost their temper or are acting out of anger or frustration, or to punish the pupil.

A calm and measured approach might not be the easiest thing to maintain in a situation that, by its very nature, could be tense and fraught. Nevertheless, knowing where you stand, what you are entitled to do and what is expected of you should go some way to helping you deal with the situation. (Again, it is worth a reminder that such incidents are not daily occurrences.)

Most of the current legislation and advice is still largely based on the Education and Inspections Act 2006 and new advice issued in 2012 has reinforced this. Fundamentally, the two basic principles are that reasonable force can be used to prevent pupils from hurting themselves or others, from damaging property or from causing disorder and, secondly, that in a school force is used for two main purposes – to control pupils or to restrain them. These principles still inform all policy and practice in this area. The 2012 advice is clear that 'all members of school staff have a legal power to use reasonable force' although, as ever, we should be mindful of the fact that such power is, ultimately, as devolved by the head teacher. It should also be noted that this power falls upon you not just on school premises, but anywhere else where you have lawful control of any pupils, such as an outing or a trip.

But for all of the above, my strong suspicion is that the main concern of the majority of teachers would be: 'What if I, personally, do not feel capable of exercising physical restraint or do not have the confidence, in a given situation, to do so?' In these circumstances the law protects teachers as well as placing obligations on them. If, for example, the incident involves a large pupil – or more than one pupil – or if the teacher believes that she or he may be at risk of injury, then other pupils who may be at risk should be removed, assistance summoned from a colleague and, until such assistance arrives, the teacher should attempt to defuse the situation orally and try to prevent the incident from escalating. Obviously, doing nothing and waiting for situations to fizzle out is simply not an option, and such an unwise approach is not only negligent in general terms but, more significantly, in legal ones as well. The DfE website states that, 'There is a power, not a duty, to use force so members of staff have discretion whether or not to use it. However, teachers and other school staff have a duty of care towards their pupils and it might be argued that failing to take action (including a failure to use reasonable force) may in some circumstances breach that duty.'

The next tricky area is one where no law can be comprehensive or definitive. Once a teacher has made a decision to intervene physically, the nature of that intervention is potentially problematic. The following abridged extracts from the DfE 2012 advice are useful up to a point:

- The term 'reasonable force' covers the broad range of actions used by most teachers at some point in their career that involve a degree of physical contact with pupils.
- Force is usually used either to control or restrain. This can range from guiding a pupil to safety by the arm through to more extreme circumstances such as breaking up a fight or where a student needs to be restrained to prevent violence or injury.
- 'Reasonable in the circumstances' means using no more force than is needed.
- Schools generally use force to control pupils and to restrain them. Control means either passive physical contact, such as standing between pupils or blocking a pupil's path, or active physical

contact such as leading a pupil by the arm out of a classroom.
- Restraint means to hold back physically or to bring a pupil under control. It is typically used in more extreme circumstances, for example when two pupils are fighting and refuse to separate without physical intervention.
- School staff should always try to avoid acting in a way that might cause injury, but in extreme cases it may not always be possible to avoid injuring the pupil.

Clearly, the law cannot unequivocally prescribe exactly what is required in every situation. The age and strength of the children involved are principal determinants as, of course, is the degree of risk or danger arising from a particular event. We have spoken before of reasonableness, and this concept comes into play here, as well as that of proportionality. We have to hope that we can get through our careers without having to use any form of physical restraint – and we've already touched on the concept of what is reasonable and what is not – but if the worst comes to the worst, the law does then give us some clear 'dos and don'ts'.

If absolutely necessary you may consider:	But don't even think about:
Physically interposing yourself between pupils	Holding around the neck or restricting breathing
Holding	Slapping, punching or kicking
Pushing	Twisting or forcing limbs
Leading by the hand or arm	Tripping
Shepherding by placing a hand in the centre of the back	Holding by the hair or ear (older colleagues may remember this as being practically compulsory for some teachers)
Using restrictive holds in extreme circumstances	Holding a pupil face down on the ground

The measures listed above may also be used in a preventative way, again only where absolutely necessary – for example, in order to stop a child from running onto a road or from throwing something.

Teachers should always avoid touching or restraining pupils in any way that may be considered indecent.

To reiterate an earlier point, in the heat of the moment it may not be possible to make finely nuanced judgements, but knowing beforehand that our actions must be informed by the immovable principles of safety, responsibility and reasonableness should help to prevent ourselves from getting into trouble as well as protecting against claims of negligence.

All serving teachers, at whatever stage in their career, should ensure that they have been given the correct information and know the procedures relating to their particular school. As always, the law will protect where it can, but ignorance is not a defence against accusations of negligence.

Capability, appraisal and disciplinary procedures

> For far too long schools have been tangled up in complex red tape when dealing with teachers who are struggling. That is why our reforms focus on giving schools the responsibility to deal with this issue fairly and quickly. Schools need to be able to dismiss more quickly those teachers who, despite best efforts, do not perform to the expected standard. Future employers also need to know more about the strengths and weaknesses of teachers they are potentially employing. Nobody benefits when poor teaching is tolerated. It puts pressure on other teachers and undermines children's education.
>
> Michael Gove, Secretary of State for Education, 2011

One can understand the anxiety of anyone, be it a parent, colleague, head teacher or even a minister of state at the thought of an incompetent teacher in charge of any class. But if ever there was an instance of tilting at windmills, the great fuss over dealing with incompetent teachers really is a case in point. In 1995 Chris Woodhead, then head of OFSTED, claimed that there were some 15,000 incompetent teachers operating in our schools – around 5% of the teaching force. Woodhead had no statistical evidence to substantiate his claim, but it was one that penetrated deep into the consciousness of politicians and members of the public alike. So what is the truth about this particular issue and how likely is it to affect you?

Before we look at the legal position, let us attempt to get some notion of the extent of the problem. In 2002 the University of Manchester published research which demonstrated that, of the total teaching force, only some 1.2 per cent ever reached the point where their performance gave their managers cause for concern. Only 0.67 per cent reached the point where managers had to move to the invoking of actual procedures. Of this 0.67 per cent,

Capability or disciplinary?

Sometimes the lines between these two areas are a little blurred but, generally speaking, this rough set of examples should help you to see that there is a difference.

Capability (sometimes called 'competence' to distinguish it from health and disability matters) procedures generally stem from the performance of an individual as a class teacher: problematic subject knowledge, failing to mark and assess properly, late completion of reports and, perhaps most frequently, very poor classroom management, are the most frequent areas for concern.

Disciplinary procedures, which deal with conduct up to and including gross misconduct, deal with areas such as theft and fraud, false claims, discriminatory behaviour, abuse of drugs or alcohol affecting the completion of professional duties, or the deliberate failure to carry out an instruction from the school's managers.

But do remember ... fewer than one in every hundred teachers ever fall foul of such procedures!

ultimately some 50 per cent resigned and around 30 per cent improved. You don't need to be a mathematical genius to calculate that of some 400,000 teachers working in England, there are not the hordes of incompetents conjured up by Woodhead. (0.67 per cent of 400,000 is 2,680, to save you diving for your calculator). In 2010 *The Times Education Supplement*, using the Freedom of Information Act, gleaned from local authorities the information that, broadly speaking, these percentages had remained pretty well constant. Research also demonstrated that, on average, the completion of proceedings took some eighteen months: whether or not this is fair and quick, as Mr Gove recommends, is a matter of opinion.

When it comes to the use of disciplinary proceedings against teachers covering, for example, allegations of misconduct as opposed to incompetence, there is no reliable research. Nevertheless, although such cases are uncommon, many that fall into the category of misconduct – and especially that of gross misconduct – often go beyond the remit of the school's own procedures.

The first thing to take into account is that in the unlikely event of your being on the wrong end of these procedures, unless your misdemeanours mean that you have, in fact, broken the law, their application is in-house and will not involve agencies outside education. The procedures that a school chooses to use are not prescribed by law; they will usually be modelled on advice given by local authorities which, in turn, will have taken into account advice from the DfE. (In the case of schools of a religious nature, it is likely that the ruling bodies of the religious organisations to which they have affiliation will have made some contribution to the formulation of regulations and policies.)

It simply cannot be emphasised too strongly that the majority of day-to-day disputes or concerns about performance are dealt with on an informal level with matters resolved and all parties moving on. However, if this does not happen informally, all procedures to be used – and schools must have such procedures by law – need to be open, transparent and fair. Although there are probably hundreds of sets of such procedures, there will only be occasional differences of emphasis between them, and all of them must allow for the following:

- Any teacher accused of failure of competence or of a disciplinary offence must be furnished with a set of the procedures that are to be used at the outset of any proceedings
- Teachers finding themselves in such a position have the right to be accompanied by a friend or trade union representative at every stage of the proceedings
- The procedures must make it clear what the process is in terms of time limits, hearings and potential outcomes
- The right to appeal must be included in all such procedures

Do bear in mind that the terms 'hearings', 'procedures', and 'appeals', as intimidating as they sound, do not mean that these instances are 'tried' in a court of law. Hearings themselves usually take place on school premises, and any judgements are made by members of the school's governing bodies. Although it is just possible in the event of gross misconduct that such hearings may end up in dismissal, a much more common outcome is a warning of some sort along with the establishment of a period of time during which improvements have to be made or issues addressed. It is also part of the school's duty of care to ensure that support is put in place in order to effect such improvements.

The plain fact is that, should you be unfortunate enough to find yourself embroiled in such a situation, you would need to take immediate advice from your trade union or professional association (bear in mind that you won't be able to join retrospectively in such circumstances). Leafing through unfamiliar documents about proceedings and hearings at a time of great stress and uncertainty is the last thing anyone would need to be doing.

What of your conduct outside school? By the time you are first appointed you will have completed the necessary paperwork through the Disclosure and Barring Service (the amalgamation of the Criminal Records Bureau [CRB] and the ISA – the Independent Safeguarding Authority). This will show any acquittals, non-convictions or convictions that you may have as well as any other information that the police have that they believe is relevant to whether you are appointed. Failure to complete this honestly, no matter how minor the offence, may well result in disciplinary procedures from the school that could, in turn, lead to dismissal.

Once in service, it goes without saying that any criminal offence committed by you will be dealt with by the law in the usual way: but what view will the school take of this, and what actions might your employers take? Obviously, the most significant factor here is the seriousness of the offence itself. The sort of minor indiscretions perpetrated by younger and less experienced teachers outside school are, more often than not, thoughtless episodes of misbehaviour which usually merit a small fine and a great deal of embarrassment. It is possible that your employer might take a position on this, especially if the misdemeanour has gone into the public domain (and it's worth remembering earlier comments about the need for great discretion around the use of social networking sites here). The school may simply choose to issue an informal word of warning; but if it chooses instead to pursue the matter and invoke disciplinary procedures, you would need to follow the advice given earlier in this section.

Perhaps the most far-reaching change to legislation since the first edition of this book in 2007 is the link between the Teachers' Standards and appraisal which was brought in by the 2010 coalition government. The effect of this is that the Standards were applicable from September 2012 to those teachers making a threshold application, being assessed for QTS or in any appraisal planning meetings where that cycle begins on or after that date – effectively, pretty well everyone. Although academies could be exempted from this obligation, the fact that OFSTED will consider the extent to which Standards have been met in all the schools they inspect, including academies, means that, in effect, academies will also be obliged to stick with the process.

The 2012 legislation links, for the first time, the appraisal process with capability procedures and, along with this, proposes a much shorter period within that capability process for teachers to demonstrate improvement. Protection that was in place to prevent numerous observations has been removed and, should you fall foul of meeting the Standards, the head or governors are now able to identify as many further objectives to meet – beyond those identified in the Standards themselves – as they see fit.

Despite the rather hostile tone and intent of some of this new legislation, it is, as always, worth maintaining a sense of proportion. Regrettably, some schools will espouse this new system of linking appraisal, the Standards and capability and indulge in bureaucratic, lumbering processes as they implement it. But, fortunately, most will not. It is significant that all the teacher trade unions have issued broadly similar advice about how this new system could operate in a way that need not be too intrusive and threatening – although we should, I think, be in little doubt that it is, indeed, designed to intrude and threaten. And to repeat one of the central messages of this book, if this new regime of scrutiny and observation isn't enough to make you join a teacher trade union, I fear for your health and sanity.

Protecting children from abuse

Legal responsibility for child protection rests with local authorities, schools and colleges: schools have a legal duty to assist local authority social service departments acting on behalf of children in need or enquiring into allegations of child abuse. Once again, this legislation stems from the Children Act 1989 and is further supported by the Education Act 2002, which obliges schools and colleges to have regard to the promotion of the welfare and safety of all children. As well as this, of course, the statutory duty of care discussed earlier places obligations on schools and teachers.

The phrase 'child protection' is a weighty one and its very mention is an indication that we are going into an area that is delicate and potentially disconcerting. In the light of this, it is worth carefully unpicking the structures and procedures that must be in place in every school as it is these, above all else, which form the foundation of how we approach this subject.

In every school there must be a member of staff with designated responsibilities for child protection. This individual is pivotal – and if you're reading this guide as a trainee, a newly qualified teacher (NQT) or a relatively inexperienced member of staff, then it certainly shouldn't be you. However, it is your responsibility to ensure that you know who this person is in your school. It is the job of this designated individual to ensure the application of local, regulatory and statutory requirements, in order that all legal obligations in this area are met.

Under no circumstances should you, personally, make any attempt to investigate any suspicions you may have about potential abuse. Any such suspicions must be reported to the designated member of staff, using the agreed procedures within the school. Furthermore, once you have reported any suspicions in the agreed manner, you should not pursue the matter in any way unless specifically directed to do so by the designated teacher: to do so could be potentially damaging to all parties, including you.

In terms of the detection of abuse, some signs such as physical manifestations or changes of behaviour on the part of the pupil may be reasonably obvious. On occasion a pupil may write something or produce a piece of work that may give you cause for alarm: in the event of such a concern, it is your legal duty to report it in the appropriate way. It is also sometimes in the nature of the job that a pupil may confide in you, asking you to keep a matter confidential. It is critical for you to understand that you cannot undertake to maintain such confidentiality should a child ask you to do so, and you must make that absolutely plain to the child.

Until such time as you choose to be the designated member of staff with responsibility for child protection, you will have fulfilled your duty of care by acquainting yourself with the procedures, key personnel and policies within your particular school, and by then acting accordingly.

But what about the real nightmare ...

.... of the accusation against you?

TV dramas in which the central plot revolves around a malicious allegation of abuse against a teacher or someone else who stands to lose everything as a result are usually very gripping and provoke morbid fascination in their viewers, but, as we know, good drama doesn't always reflect the rather more mundane facts of such situations in real life. So, in keeping with the sense of perspective that I have tried to maintain throughout this guide, let us just look at the extent of the problem.

A House of Commons Report from 2009, drawing on evidence from teacher unions and other agencies including Childline and the NSPCC, finds that the number of allegations against teachers remains fairly constant year on year at around 2,000 per annum. Of these cases the percentage found to have significant substance averages out at around 3% – effectively, around 60 people per year out of a teaching force of around 400,000. Put another way, the number of allegations against teachers ending in prosecution is statistically insignificant at around 1 in 6,600. Which is fine, just as long as you're not the one who is accused.

There is little doubt that being such a victim is traumatic in the extreme, and it is in such cases that the whole idea of the law affording teachers rights as well as responsibilities comes into play. In the rare event of your being the victim of a malicious allegation, there are a few things that it is vital to remember.

Does every child still matter?

In 2003 the government introduced the Every Child Matters initiative following the high-profile case of the death of a child, Victoria Climbie, who had clearly been failed by a number of public bodies. The desired outcomes of the scheme were defined as the need for every child to:

- Be healthy
- Stay safe
- Enjoy and achieve
- Make a positive contribution
- Achieve economic wellbeing

The dedicated website for the scheme outlined its purpose in the following way:

> This means that the organisations involved with providing services to children – from hospitals and schools, to police and voluntary groups – will be teaming up in new ways, sharing information and working together, to protect children and young people from harm and help them achieve what they want in life. Children and young people will have far more say about issues that affect them as individuals and collectively.

But is the scheme still 'live'? The coalition government shows little enthusiasm for it and it is difficult to find on the DfE website. The current secretary of state is on record in parliament as saying that he doubts the importance of the outcomes listed above in that not 'many Members of Parliament would be able to recite them in the same way that we recite the Lord's Prayer'. Nevertheless, although no longer part of any official documentation, many schools and local authorities still choose to have regard for the aims of Every Child Matters.

The first of these is to contact your trade union or professional association without delay (as mentioned earlier, it is worth bearing in mind that most such organisations will not permit you to join retrospectively – especially, of course, as such cases could be protracted and use a great deal of time and expertise). Secondly, you must be furnished with a copy of the procedures under which the school is acting and, obviously, you will need to read these and ask questions of your union official. Thirdly, say and do absolutely nothing until advised to do so: although it may be difficult, you need to adopt the attitude of the hard-faced criminals of TV drama who stay entirely mute until their brief arrives.

There is, regrettably, little to lighten such incidents. Police and social services may be mentioned and could even become involved, and that, in itself, is worrying and unnerving for anyone. However, a highly developed, well-refined and thorough system means that the stuff of teachers' nightmares rarely becomes reality. The widespread public debate in recent years has led many people to believe that the rights of accusers outweigh those of the accused in such situations: fortunately, statistics and facts belie that belief. Nonetheless, as with so much of what we've already covered, the trick is to be forewarned and forearmed. The law protects you, the teacher, as much as it does children, and the best thing that you can do is to ensure that you are aware of agreed procedures and practices in your school, thereby ensuring that the chances of your being liable remain extremely slim.

Special educational needs

The world of education has undergone many shifts in the last twenty years, but few have been so profound as the way in which we deal with children with special educational needs (SEN). From a position in many schools where a few children were herded off into a separate room under the supervision of 'the remedial teacher', SEN is now at the heart of most schools' practice. The SEN Code of Practice came into effect in 2002 and is one of the few pieces of documentation and advice untouched by the coalition government that came to power in 2010. It is clear that academies must also have regard to the Code.

One casualty of the overhaul of policy by the 2010 government was the TeacherNet website which is now subsumed into that of the DfE. Nonetheless, the outline from that site still provides us with a comprehensive overview of what the Code requires of every school:

- to decide the school's SEN policy and approach, setting up appropriate staffing and funding arrangements and oversee the school's work
- to do its best to ensure that the necessary provision is made for any pupil who has a special need
- to ensure that teachers in the school are aware of the importance of identifying and providing for those pupils who have SEN
- to ensure that a pupil with SEN joins in the activities of the school, together with pupils who do not have SEN, as far as is reasonably practical
- to report to parents on the implementation of the school's policy for pupils with SEN and notify them when SEN provision is being made for their child

- to have regard to the Code of Practice when carrying out duties towards all pupils with SEN
- to appoint a 'responsible person', who makes sure that all those who work with a child with a statement of SEN are told about the statement

The 'responsible person' of the last bullet point is usually called the Special Educational Needs Co-ordinator, or SENCO. Some schools have now added the word 'disability' to the title, reflecting a clearer concern for the needs of those children with specific disabilities. It is through the SEN(D)CO that most information and necessary documentation is routed. Whilst it is true that it is upon this person that the majority of these obligations will fall, you, as an individual teacher, must also absorb the information and background you have been given about pupils, adjusting your own practice accordingly.

The legal status of the SEN Code of Practice which, like all DfE circulars and publications is available online, is interesting and illuminating. The penultimate bullet point above refers to schools having 'regard' to the Code. What this means is that although the implementation of the Code is not, in fact, a legal requirement, schools have to demonstrate that the provision made to meet the needs of children with SEN are at least as good as the guidance laid down in the Code itself. In other words, schools can devise their own practices but, in reality, few choose to stray from the advice given in the Code, which in its own preface acknowledges that some diversity of approach is necessary:

This Code of Practice is effective from 1 January 2002. From that date LEAs, schools, early education settings and those who help them – including health and social services – must have regard to it. They must not ignore it. That means that whenever settings, schools and LEAs decide how to exercise their functions relating to children with special educational needs, and whenever the health and social services provide help to settings, schools and LEAs in this, those bodies must consider what this Code says. These bodies must fulfil their statutory duties towards children with special educational needs but it is up to them to decide how to do so in the light of the guidance in this Code of Practice. The Code is designed to help them to make effective decisions but it does not – and could not – tell them what to do in each individual case.

Generally, overall provision for SEN children rests at the level of school management but, depending on your circumstances, you will almost certainly be dealing with SEN issues every day of your working life. It is most unlikely that as a subject or class teacher at the start of your career, anyone will challenge the legality of what you, personally, provide for SEN pupils (such challenges, incidentally, almost always come from parents or carers). It is, however, a matter of contractual obligation on your part to ensure that proper provision is made in your classes for all pupils.

Anti-discrimination and human rights

Low expectations of pupils by teachers often seem based on a stereotypical view that White/Caribbean (mixed heritage) pupils have fragmented home backgrounds and 'confused' identities. These pupils often experience racism from teachers and from their White and Black peers targeted at their mixed heritage.

Research from Tikly *et al.,* University of Nottingham

Racism is still a reality in the life of some minority ethnic student teachers/trainees. HEIs [Higher Education Institutions] and partnership schools have an equal opportunities policy, but not a separate antiracism policy.

from the Multiverse website, which provided teachers and student teachers/trainees with a range of resources focusing on the educational achievement of pupils from diverse backgrounds

It is not necessary to prove that the other person intended to discriminate against you: you only have to show that you received less favourable treatment as a result of what they did.

Advice from the Equality and Human Rights Commission

The law prohibits discrimination on the grounds of sex, race, age, sexual orientation, religion or belief and disability. The law governing these areas now resides principally in the Equality Act of 2010.

The idea that, as you gear yourself up to do battle with your rowdy Year 10s or to juggle the various needs of your mixed Year 5s, you ought to just quickly check the requirements of the Equality Act 2010 may seem a tad unrealistic.

All the same, the fact that this legislation does, indeed, apply to schools means that we have to treat these matters with great seriousness.

We should start by saying that, in the last three decades or so, most schools have been in the forefront of the battle against discrimination of all sorts. No one in their right mind would pretend that the situation is perfect, and the comment about the experience of trainee teachers at the start of this section is alarming and depressing. However, most schools do have anti-discrimination policies and these are reinforced by classroom practice. It is also true to say that the implementation and monitoring of these policies within schools will fall, in most cases, to senior managers and experienced teachers: for the time being, we will limit ourselves to looking at what a new entrant to the profession needs to know.

Let us make the clear and unequivocal statement that it is unlawful to discriminate against a pupil on the grounds of sex, race, colour, nationality, ethnicity or national origins. Similarly, it is unlawful to discriminate on the grounds of sexual orientation, religion or belief. Transgender issues fall within the bounds of sex discrimination. These principles are clear-cut and non-contestable.

Most, if not all, teachers would be horrified at the idea of discriminating against any pupils in such a way. However, the law about discrimination is not as straightforward as we might like it to be. Although there are obvious forms of discrimination such as abusive comments, others are not as immediately apparent. The low expectations referred to above, along with such things as subtle differences in assessment and provision, can be construed as discrimination – albeit that these things can be unwittingly done, and sometimes with the best of intentions. How might this happen?

It is at this point that we hit the most difficult and by far the most contentious area when it comes to discriminatory behaviour. There are few of us who would expend too much sympathy on the teacher who makes racist or sexist jibes, but it does become much more difficult to unpick whether or not our actions have had the *effect* of being discriminatory, although we had not intended them to be so. The important factor for both direct and indirect discrimination is described in the EHRC quotation at the start of this section: irrespective of whether there is *intent* to discriminate, it is the *outcome* that is important.

What does this mean in our classrooms? A good place to begin is to look at the question of cultural bias in questions used to assess students' abilities. The issue of cultural bias has raged in the educational world for decades and is best illustrated by looking at the old Eleven Plus exam, which was used to determine what sort of secondary schools pupils would attend. A significant part of the examination was based on IQ tests, in themselves a theatre of war for academics and educationalists. Questions would, for example, show incomplete pictures of a tennis court or a house and ask what was missing. The required answers would be, respectively, the net and the chimney: but it's not difficult to see the cultural specificity of such questions – such crude examples are much rarer now, of course, but they exemplify what we mean by cultural bias. The materials used in our classrooms today have been produced and designed by teachers to avoid such obvious pitfalls, but vigilance is required to avoid falling into the trap of indirect discrimination.

On a broader scale – one which will probably not impact on the lives of newly qualified or inexperienced teachers – we can examine how a school, as an institution, can be guilty of indirect discrimination. That is when the same rule is applied to all, but its impact on a protected group is very different to the impact on others. In a case heard by the House of Lords, a school's insistence that all boys wear a cap as part of the school uniform was clearly discriminatory against Sikhs and was deemed to be unjustifiable on educational grounds. Beyond this, a school needs to ensure that its admission and application policies do not fall foul of the law, as well as ensuring that its exclusion rates do not demonstrate significant bias.

As usual, we need to look at what all of this means for you: the teacher at the start of their career. And, once again, it comes down to being acquainted with the policies and practices of your particular school, which should, if properly formulated and effectively applied, work towards the elimination of discrimination and prejudice where you work.

It would be extremely naïve to think that schools are completely free of such discrimination. Regrettably, we sometimes become acutely aware of the fact that racist and sexist attitudes are far from rare in our classrooms, school corridors, and, yes, our staffrooms. It may also be extremely difficult for you as a new and relatively inexperienced member of staff to raise such concerns in a public way, and it is likely that you will need to consider which line manager or senior member of staff to approach about the existence of discriminatory behaviour. Two principles should always underlie your actions. Firstly, ensure that your own professional practice is non-discriminatory in every aspect of what you do. Secondly, consult your trade union or professional association when you have anxieties in this area: if that body is not vigorous when addressing matters of discrimination, change and join one that is.

But it's not a problem in our school ...

In his introduction to a 2004 DfES publication *Aiming High: Understanding the Educational Needs of Minority Ethnic Pupils in Mainly White Schools*, the then Parliamentary Under Secretary of State for Schools, Stephen Twigg, wrote:

> Our aim is to help the schools in mainly white areas to create an environment where all pupils have access to a curriculum which embraces the range of cultural backgrounds across the country, where all teachers are aware of the needs of a particular group of pupils, and where the school workforce is equipped to meet the needs of a diverse learning community.

It might be very easy to think there is 'no problem' in your particular school, but to adopt such an attitude is both to invite accusations of indirect discrimination as well as being in dereliction of your professional duty of care. Racist attitudes, if unchallenged, can harden and become 'acceptable' in such an environment. The same goes for attitudes to disability and, in single-sex schools, uncontested remarks of an offensive or prejudicial nature about the opposite sex.

Current legislation works to ensure that all forms of prejudice are eliminated from our schools, but the legislation does more than just place a duty upon schools to prohibit discrimination. It emphasises the obligation to promote race equality and equality of opportunity. Hence, an attitude of 'no problem here' simply will not wash.

With regard to the issue of disability, the Equality Act makes it unlawful to discriminate against disabled pupils, including those who may be making applications to attend the school. It is fairly obvious that in a situation where not all schools are equipped to deal with all pupils with disabilities, the responsibility for overall provision of access lies with local authorities; but within schools themselves the same approach to equality of opportunity in relation to sex or race applies to disability.

Finally, remember that laws proscribing discrimination protect you, the teacher, as well as the pupil. In terms of recruitment, promotion and access to benefits and services, it is illegal for employers to discriminate on the grounds of race, sex, age, marital status, sexual orientation, religion or belief, disability, transgender status, trade union membership or activity, or by reason of part-time employment or fixed-term contract. As well as this, employers are bound by law to ensure that procedures are in place for complaints by staff to be pursued. However, a word of caution should be added here: pursuing complaints as an individual could be a difficult, time-consuming and, ultimately, very dispiriting business. To do so without the advice and support of a trade union or professional association is not recommended, even for the most experienced of us.

So, to recap …

I hope that the big messages of this guide have now become clear: if not, here is the digested version:

- For most teachers in the normal course of events, it is not necessary to know a great deal about the law and how it affects you, although knowing the precise nature of what is meant by 'duty of care', along with your contractual obligations, is very important
- The number of teachers who fall foul of the law when conducting their professional duties is almost statistically insignificant
- Acquainting yourself with the policies and procedures in your particular school, and applying these consistently, is easily the best way of protecting yourself against accusations of negligence or abuse
- Joining a trade union or professional association is vital. Joining your subject association is also highly recommended

I would be surprised if some trainee teachers or others new to the profession were not just a touch sceptical about some of the points made in the guide. What if, for example, there are no policies about behaviour, health and safety, physical restraint, or any of the other areas we've touched on, readily available in the school? And do you, as a new and inexperienced member of staff, really want to draw attention to yourself by asking to see such documents if they're not easily to be found? Might it seem a little strange if, on your first day, you were to ask to know who was the lead professional for child protection? Are you ready to be the first one to point out that parental consent to detention is not required, or that in loco parentis is an outdated and fairly useless concept?

There are no glib answers here, but there are a few things that you might want to consider. The first of these would be to try to ascertain at interview

whether there are basic behaviour management policies in place and, most importantly, whether there are arrangements made for the induction of new staff where questions about policies will be dealt with and key personnel will be identified. (Incidentally, an induction programme is an entitlement for teachers in their NQT year, although there are no stipulations about the form that this should take.) The sort of answers you receive to these enquiries may well be instrumental in reaching a decision about whether that particular school is for you.

There is an ongoing joke amongst those of us who have made teacher trade unionism part of our lives about how we got ourselves involved. It starts with a simple question at a staff meeting about why the heating is so temperamental or whether refreshments can be provided on those evenings when staff need to stay late, and it ends with you being the school union representative and, most likely, a place on your local union committee. Although there is a deal of folklore about trade union membership being a barrier to promotion and advancement, there is not much evidence to support this. The law is absolutely unequivocal in ensuring that membership of a trade union and promoting its activities as a representative or an officer cannot be used as reason for discriminating against a teacher in matters of employment, promotion, redundancy or dismissal. The Employment Rights Act 1996 enshrines these rights in law. What is more, there is plenty of evidence to show that a willingness to engage with such issues often goes hand-in-glove with a clear understanding of the major educational issues of the day – and that can be a real advantage when going for promoted posts. True professionalism is about knowing how the law works for you – and even helping to frame it – as well as recognising how it works for our pupils.